Springtime Rhapsody

Springtime Rhapsody

UMASANKAR VADREVU

(Introducing Gaurika Mehrotra)

PARTRIDGE

ISBN: Hardcover   978-1-4828-8371-8
       Softcover   978-1-4828-8370-1
       eBook   978-1-4828-8369-5

To order additional copies of this book, contact
Partridge India
000 800 10062 62
orders.india@partridgepublishing.com

www.partridgepublishing.com/india

Acknowledgements

thank you Sangsy for being that
one good friend and
giving your feedback
at all times

and

Scarlett I can't thank you enough
for your reviews and to be saying
what you think as a reader

This book is dedicated to
the dashing and lovely
young Anvit Singh Khurana
Born on 29th September 2014
Who left us for the heavenly abode on
6th February 2016

You shall be forever in our hearts

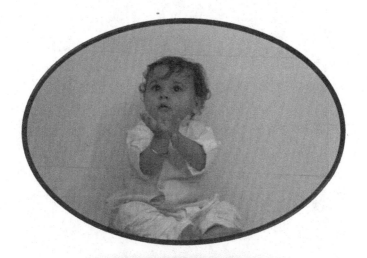

Contents

About the Poet

Umasankar Vadrevu

The poet seems to unwind his thoughts; words seem to flow passionately, merging with each other. The intricacies of life, love and nature seem ensconced within the poet himself. These thoughts flow like breeze in a valley, carrying with it various smells of the land giving an elusive effervescence in the form of poetry.

Overview

Poetry of life cannot be more simply and easily penned down by anyone else more adeptly. Words seem to flow from his mind like dew drops from the heavens above. Every single poem depicts a new perception of life in the best form. The depiction through his poetry encompasses all emotions in a true feeling.

The poet spends most of his working time in the barren deserts of the Middle East. He keeps spinning splendid poetry and brings everyone to wonder the very way his senses have developed. Be it poetry of nature or about friends, lovers or children he has a very distinct signature.

He has explored and moved in his career from the heat of the foundries to the oil fields from the toughest to the worst terrains. In his spare time he loves to spend time in his own country in the lap of nature. He has developed an innate ability to be able to write some of his best works in the most arid regions of the world.

A few of his works are from his earlier written time somewhere in the late eighties. One of his most recent attempts at writing about the demi god Krishna has been very good. His next book is on "Immoral Trafficking of Children". He also plans at writing a poetry book exclusively on the mythological stories and on foundries but in some time. This may only happen in the next couple of years.

He is in this book introducing two young poetesses Scarlett Pragya and the other in a little girl Gaurika Mehrotra.

This reverse book comprising of two books Springtime Rhapsody by Umasankar Vadrevu and M@dness and Musings by Scarlett Pragya is the second in the series of books he plans to publish. His first published book is "Life Through A Prism".

Rain

The rain it came pouring down,
Crashing through the trees, all around,
Lightning struck and thunder crashed,
Tree's they got excited; bowing and swinging,
Tossing and swirling, cleansed the dust within,
Clouds they growled, with a constant rumble,
Cooling the water, all the layers around,
A sheet that formed an icy cold layer,
Lightning struck and it crashed right below.
Rivulets of rain water rolling down,
The crashing, booming and rushing of water,
Wild gusts blowing the trees around,
Ecstatic as it was, just like a forest in worship,
Nature in its enthusiastic and innate glory
Caused a celebration of humans with Gods!

Twenty Ninth December 2015
Chennai, India

Uzma

Thoughts so simple,
Never endingly sweet,
Mesmerising eyes they just have been,
Richness in thought, captivating looks
The eyes as they auger,
In severance of gaze,
Touched upon the mortal being,
Sitting next, as the flight it began to roll,
Patiently yes an ear plug moves,
To the ear and the music begins,
Sound waves travel to the portals of her brain,
Hypnotised by the music she sat,
Face blank thoughtless,
Until the moment of provocation,
Thoughts unfurl,
Voice modulations hit the perfect chord,
A new friendship begins,
A new journey forged,
As the flight it touched down
Thoughts they merge,
Just like a roller coaster ride,
On a new wave it spread its wings,
A surge on to new heights,

Springtime Rhapsody

Levels unknown, here we are,
Monstrously construed,
A generation apart, but life is,
All but a new hope!

Tenth October 2015
Majnoon
@ Lunch time with songs of Richard Clayderman
Playing the 50 Greatest Piano Hits

Umasankar Vadrevu

The Banana Leaf

Heavy as it would,
I needed a shelter from the shower
I knew it would be, but once again,
Very cold, if I don't find a cover

Lo there stood a banana plant,
Leaves low down for me to uphold,
The plant actually was luckily in a slant,
I wonder if it would another shower hold

Springtime Rhapsody

But fingers crossed I used it as a cover,
Held on top of my head already wet,
For some safety and it stood tall as a tower,
If it had rained any longer, I would have there, itself slept.

Life does bring many wonders,
The glow of the leaf shone on the face,
A contrast of life so much with splendour
I love this country and I love this place!

First May 2015
Majnoon

Krishna

As he was born unto Earth,
The year was BC three thousand one hundred and twelve,
His birth is also called Sri Jayanth
As from now on, on this story I would delve

The birth more than five thousand years old,
The story of this little child once forlorn,
Krishna the man god, his tale many times told,
And in a stony prison this little child was born

Springtime Rhapsody

Salutations O' Krishna, my supreme lord,
The dweller of our hearts, everything Absolute,
The Soul of this universe, in one word - God,
Who took a human form and life with him is so resolute.

I bow to that para-brahman, as this universe,
With him alone is it with-held,
Without whom life is so very adverse,
Krishna my lord, in our hearts you do dwell.

An incarnation of the great Vishnu
The purna avatara, a perfect incarnation
Adorned with sixteen rays, this god of Hindu
Someone as beautiful found in no other Nation

His enchanting form with flute in hand
Is a form that pours out devotion,
Enchanting notes that pour out playing as he stands,
An embodiment of great qualities without a notion

The towering genius of his age
Glorious and extraordinary,
His teachings, brilliant in every page,
Momentous import to humanity in many ways

His foster parents, by a cruel king Kamsa, were harried
On the pretext of killing the eighth born child,
He killed the first six, the seventh miscarried,
The eighth baby after birth the story grew wild.

The guards they fell asleep totally magical,
Chains, Shackles and locks automatically opened,
The child taken through, the river which was hysterical,
To be exchanged with a girl child chosen.

As the fated morning rose into light,
The prison walls heard the wails,
The cruel king without seeing the plight,
Threw on a rock, the girl child frail

Without hitting the rock she rose high above,
A voice high up boomed, Krishna is alive,
The king fell to the ground in painful remorse,
And their life he then tried to revive

Released their shackles and washed their feet,
The ministerial advice, all the newborns to die
The king killed all new born on that day indiscrete,
The killing took place amidst a huge hue and cry.

Yashoda and Nanda found Krishna as their son,
Religious ceremonies performed in secrecy,
The wrath of Kamsa was avoided on this one,
Everything done in instant spontaneity

Taught by Sandipani, a sage of Avantipura,
He inspired his classmates with love,
Lured all gopis with his blessed lila,
His nature as soft as the breast of a dove

Everyone was consulted including Gargamuni,
Your Son he said is a, "Supreme Personality",
Life in the village then became very sunny,
This little boy played with Kamsa's brutality

The first of the lot was Putana to attempt;
Died having life being sucked out of her;
She tried her best to brutally tempt;
Eyes blurred, voice slurred and soul went out in a whir.

After Putana died, the villagers were mesmerised,
As such a little boy had done the deed and killed;
For his protection performed auspicious rites,
All the pretty Gopi's for him formed a guild!

Nala Kubera and Manigreeva turned to trees by curse,
Bala Krishna stood between them and did uproot,
The siddhas came out liberated and sang a verse,
They praised the lord and heavenwards did shoot.

The fruit selling woman called out aloud,
Krishna in his innocence a handful of sand did give,
In exchange filled his hands with fruit he was proud,
In her basket the sand turned into gems she saw it live!

Snake demon Aghasura, looked like a mountain cave,
Expanded himself to a snake of length eight miles,
Krishna considered to first all his friends save,
And then grew to sizes huge to kill the snake vile

Brahma's kidnapping misdeed was unheard,
Until he chose to become cruel unbeknown
However Krishna with his wonder powers substituted,
Himself for the families of the kidnapped children

Just like children Krishna was naughty to the core,
While the mothers watched enjoying the fun,
He played around in mud till everything got sore,
Bodies getting tanned fully in the hot sun

The pranks went so high that it once hit the roof,
The mother was angry and tied him to a grinding stone,
But would it stop everything, No! It increased the spoof,
The butter thieves, their mothers, never did condone

Sri Krishna said this once to Uddhava
Give no attention to people, who ridicule,
Prostrate on the ground bow to the Chandala,
Remember everyone is a mere miniscule!

The flute is the symbol of Pranava,
This attracted the maids of Vraja,
To meet their lord on the banks of Yamuna,
The music sweeter than the bliss of moksha

The love of the gopis towards Krishna,
Was divine love unlike union of sexes; the aspiration,
Jivatman to merge in paramatma
Merging of souls without perspiration

Springtime Rhapsody

The forest was lovely and charming,
Water clear while the wind was blowing,
Cowherds entered it was heartwarming,
Rapturous notes playing and the cows mooing!

The meritorious flute kept playing,
Touched by the nectar of the Lord's lips,
Water nourishing and the plants thrilling,
As the Lotus feet move, an insect in happiness flips.

The music so enthralling feels like Heaven's on earth,
The peacocks dance creating a splash of splendour,
In Brindavan the feeling of love sees no dearth,
Clouds appear and rainbows drench the sky in colour

The reason to offer sacrifices to Indira was unbeknown,
Krishna reasoned out why sacrifices are not meant to be
Everyone born unto earth had a predetermined life span,
The reasoning the king and the fellow man began to see

Thus stopped the offerings to Lord Indira,
The god of rain now angered to the core,
Did not like the way Krishna explained nature and Karma
Collected all clouds and then began a huge downpour

Winds and Rain, thunder and hail,
Hit Brindavan for seven nights and days,
Krishna with his little finger lifted the hill,
And people of Brindavan below the hill were safe

Nanda fasting on Ekadasi and worshipped Janardana,
Went to bathe in the river Yamuna on Dvadasi
He entered the river at dead of night, a servant of Varuna,
Seized Nanda, and took him in, the devious Rakshasi

Varuna fell on Nanda's feet, and begged for pardon,
With great reverence he took Nanda to the banks,
Begged for forgiveness without pride or wanton,
Then to return to his kingdom, he slowly sank

Thus is told the story of Krishna, who;
Walked this earth for 125 years,
Love he taught amongst, living to be true,
And in the Gopi's he showed in happiness, tears!

Sage Vyasa meditating on the banks of Sarasvati,
His heart disturbed with no satisfaction and peace,
And Narada came upon his rescue; asked him to write
        on Hari,
Upon writing Srimad Bhagvatam he attained it with ease.

Bhagvata unique in beauty and charm,
Its diction and philosophy on the solace of life,
Is a valuable treasure house divine and warm,
And Bhagvatam never causes amongst men rife!

The Bhagavata consists of eighteen thousand Slokas
Three hundred and thirty-two chapters, and twelve
    Skandhas,
The tenth Skandha contains of the Lord, his Lilas
As Prabhasa, Brindavana, Mathura, Dwaraka,
    Kurukshetra and Kumaras

Lord Krishna – The Joy of Devaki,
The life of Radha, beloved of Gopis,
Here I end this tale a part of Krishna's life
The Giver of eternal bliss and peace

First May 2015
Majnoon
The Painting of Krishna has been made by Ms. Pranita Das.

Feelings

When the mind goes blank and expression is lost,
When you are in love, and you know it's in vain,
When friends seem near, but all are gone,
Then death is near, but we don't feel pain.

It feels good to write poetry, but words don't flow,
It is sad but you know, he taught me once
Saying never give up, never let go,
Give me the courage, so into life I can plunge

Life's been a bitch, life's very harsh,
I wish everything would never have fell so fast apart,
Sometimes it feels the surroundings are like a marsh,
With mine's under your feet to rip you apart

I would not mind being in a battlefield, to this,
It sucks, it pains, and feels so lonely at times,
Life certainly isn't as rosy as would seem a kiss,
But we have a life ahead, worth more than a dime!

So live your life, fully as one would say,
Live your life, in style "Kings Size",
The line above feels like a fag, any day;
But what better thing than life can you get as a prize!

23-02-2015
In John's Office
YMCA Delhi

Umasankar Vadrevu

My Placid Palace

Must you wonder a little longer?
I would be the lochness in the lake deep,
Knocking upon your door I would ask,
Baby would you care for some company!

30-01-2015
Site Majnoon, Iraq

Inflight

It spreads its wings and begins the flight,
Diving downwards from the lofty branch,
Wings wide open, without any fright,
Focused in thought, it knows it can.

Agile as it is, it leaps off in a downward flow,
The feathers unruffled, looks so soft,
Gently pulls up and in a motion slow,
A couple of flaps and it is high up and aloft

It soars and glides as it touches a thermal draft,
Then with wings spread it goes with the flow,
Colours of feathers a soft hue, God surely has a craft,
An aura, it surely has, a wonderful glow!

Observant and in a thought so deep,
I wonder what's on this new mission,
The rest of their flock, are they in sleep,
This bird in me has caused a commotion

30th January 2015
Majnoon

Innocence

Freshness to the sense, the beautiful raindrop brings,
To savor the rain, as on its journey to earth it drops,
A love with nature and innocence so sweet, it begins,
An open mouth and a tongue that sweetly pops

Innocent and sweet the face so soft,
Happiness in-exorbitant the experience,
The smell of the rain as it touches the earth,
Exhilarating the smell, nostalgic to the sense

The smell of mud as it rises in to the air,
Scintillating it remains for a time to come
The smell it's brewed from gods own lair,
And it lasts till the first rain is done

30th December 2014
Bangalore

Chandeliers

As I stood in front of the shops Galore,
Wonderstruck at the effects as I stood in awe,
In multitudes they shone all afore,
Chandeliers hundreds lit high and low

My mind as it gazes to the skies above,
Stars infinite as they shine in formations,
Millions of constellations high and low,
High above all these so called nations

Brilliance the way they hang above,
No strings, no ropes just magnetically strung,
The Milky Way looks like millions of dark coves,
Everything so awesome but also far flung!

23-12-2014
Lalit Grand Palace
Srinagar, India

A Liberated Relation

I set my foot and it hit me back,
I tried to walk, couldn't find my track,
I feel lost and helpless, isn't it sad,
Where are you my friend I need you real bad.

Life's stories are a crazy few,
Every day then seemed as fresh as dew,
It started off once on a very good note,
By God! There now are a very few on whom I dote!

Each day I look out for you my dear friend?
Life isn't as good as it seems to lend
It suddenly seems I lost the beautiful pot of gold,
And the roots seem now to be losing hold

15th Oct 2014
In the Office Majnoon

Thank You Note

I never even for a moment felt, as if I had thrust,
Into the portals of your life, it was a pleasure ride,
From the 30th of August which was in Mumbai for me the
first night,
Could any friend put his thoughts in a crazier stride?

Life's moments for me, packed into a fortnight,
Crazy it felt; but, yes we lived it right,
I am sorry Srikanth if you got the fright,
Well, it was not intended that way even a slight

I seriously wonder when and how that name it stuck,
Tweety is a wonderful child my dear, she has her way, she
has her style,
In all simplicity, I would say it's the writers luck,
She has flair with certain words, and we will get there in
a while.

Guys you were awesome in your own pretty way,
You kept your space, while you were there,
Protective you were, as you kept me at bay,
One could see it every night, on my face it glared!

I knew I was clean, no thoughts in mind,
As we sat there, connecting with every word spoken,
Srikanth I am sorry, I know I overstayed,
But thoughts they now stand highly interwoven.

Thank you guys for the time and space,
You now have a pain in the neck always at bay.

Ninth September, 2014
Priya's Home,
Mumbai,

Thoughts

My mind as it unfurls its thoughts,
In leaps and bounds it flies to nestle,
In the cradles of coursera, as it beckons
Waves they grind, like in, a mortar and pestle.

These that travel faster than light,
Through neurons triggered by electrical impulses,
Energy created in the organs held tight,
By digesting just grains of rice and pulses

I do wonder, I do think,
If all my student friends in this course can bring,
A change so large in this world very quick
That can make our mother earth sing

That! Will be a day, we can reckon
The point from where we can all surely begin,
A page fresh and warm to flip on,
Which then will become a world so Linkedin.

January 7th 2014
While doing the Coursera Course on
Energy, the Environment, and Our Future

Umasankar Vadrevu

The Wrath of Gods

The gods above were angry, and;
The clouds were getting gloomy,
Tearing through the clouds came striking,
A flash of lightning fast below,
It hit the earth; it struck with a jolt,
With tens of thousands of volts may be more
The shattering sound of clouds came,
But rather very slow

Springtime Rhapsody

It sheared a tree, burnt it through,
Half was gone, as if was never there,
Just was smoke, no heat no dust,
But cool as anything, seemingly new!
It was a sight, a rare one though,
Half gone with gods own blade,
With the blink of an eye,
A lightning flash, it was gone phew!

Life still stands, though like a curse it hit,
A tree so gigantic that stood once,
Steadfast it still holds its ground,
Mighty it seems even though half gone,
Lightning it never hits the same place twice,
If it does, it will no more be in tons,
The mighty tree in the next may sizzle and die;
 Life from its branches will run away.

January 7th 2014
Sitting in the Eye of the Storm

The Expression

It came in a thunderous dumbstruck way,
As Ray looked over the counter, and at his face,
The answer it came out with thrill and awe,
My name at last! Someone high as finally set his gaze.

The name he blurted, feeling thrilled;
Without realizing the cold blast, would eventually hit,
Dumb struck he was; his happiness killed,
Unbeknown to him, someone has now bit

Stuttered and stammered, words did not flow,
He felt paralysed, numb and pale,
Not in his usual self, death came in one blow
A wind of high velocity hit him, like a gale.

He felt tethered and life was shorn,
The hourly breaks were finally put to bed,
He felt lost and very forlorn,
The dogs of freedom left him and his sled.

Springtime Rhapsody

He sat sulking for a very long time,
Jumped and moved like a bull on the run,
Then decided with Ray to discuss his crime,
Then he said if I can't go to my room, let me go and
   catch some sun.

5th January 2014
From the Portals of my Office Desk

Popsicle

Popsicle ate an icicle and it slipped down his throat,
It dangled in his gut for some time and slipped down
      below,
Popsicle now has three testicles and ones changing sizes,
And it's melting continuously creating a huge overflow.

Popsicle felt cold below and it hurt him really sore,
His thirst for water diminished and he felt real cold,
His sac expanded and as they reglated, he was at the
      door,
Not before too long, he realized he was getting old.

January 5th 2014

Musings

Life's strange ways comes multi-pronged,
The writings on the wall with time change to graffiti
Fun things are to be carried out un-hindered,
Although the writing seems at first like spaghetti

Musical overtures are present everywhere,
Do not shut your ears to the world, but listen,
Let it with the heart romanticize bare,
Life though looking grim will also enliven.

Life encompasses many facets;
To be felt, touched and romanticized;
Some worn, torn and shredded; yet others,
Neatly dusted, pressed and vacuumised.

Life dawns upon oneself, as one is born,
Lives on, even after the human body dies,
Thoughts are like the seeds of an acorn,
And waits in the womb till it does fertlise

January 5th 2014
My room

Dawn

The girl she sits down at the hollows,
The morning sun filters through the forest brush,
Dew washed, the grass fresh and green,
The grass juicy very endearing, a reindeer it wakes up
    fresh.

The light heavenly, a blessing in the chill of the dawn air,
A promise of a bright warm day in the cold of the winter,
The moss enveloped roots, creating a carpeted lair,
On which rests the little girl, the forest ahead on a platter

A small brook, meandering, pleasantly calm,
The stream it chuckles as it falls a step below,
The antlers majestic and huge, if hits surely will slam,
But, the eyes gentle and warm, affection seems to flow.

The roots as high as her, with hair cutely plaited,
Legs crossed she sits, hands afore, she waits,
Patiently, maybe for that moment, with baited, breath;
For the reindeer to wake up from its sleepy lair

January 05th 2014
My Room

Chandeliers of the Gods

As I stood in front of the shops Galore,
In multitudes they shone all afore,
Wonderstruck at the effects as I stood in awe,
Chandeliers hundreds lit high and low

My mind as it gazes to the skies above,
Stars infinite as they shine in formations,
Millions of constellations high and low,
High above all these so called nations

They shine before a black carpeted layer,
Colourful and different sizes; are variants,
Some bright and shiny hung in vapour,
Others drop down from the garden so luxuriant.

Many brighter than the overpowering sun,
Though light years away they shine bright,
Appearing as specs in the cold air that runs,
Shall change when the magnetic waves pull tight

The black holes that are, will suck the stars,
Not only the stars, but moons planets and all,
The planetary positions once they change,
Will cause the biggest nations to fall

Astrological predictions will go for a toss,
Devastating lands, seas and mostly all,
A new world then will arise from the humble moss,
Creating a new world from them all

January 5th 2014
In the Coffee Shop

The Locust

The locust he came on slow, but came on by,
Spread his wings and tried to fly,
Without realizing they have been clipped,
And it is futile to even try.

He walked me through for breakfast one day,
To put his assumptions and doubts to bay,
He tried hard, he tried to pry,
Did not realize I was very sly.

He poured his concerns one by one,
Opened and told what he had done,
On "Tell Shell" he had registered a case,
And thought that is why you were there.

When negated and said, it can't be that,
The locust he felt, was squashed flat,
The thoughts in the mind went by leaps and bounds,
Around a new dimension his thoughts began to wound.

The next wave that came was real good,
My thoughts were craving for real food,
Out he blurted his feelings very grave,
But tried to show himself as very brave.

Oh! It was sure it was for an interview very big,
It said then, he will clip me in my wing,
But, Alas! My friend, Ahmed gave us out,
He has squeaked without a doubt.

Now he knows why you went,
To IEC my dear Friend!

29th December 2013
From the portals of my office desk

The Violinist

Colorful splurges on a canvas fresh,
Eye catching it is and I wished it were,
The beauty, my I really have a crush,
The clothing she wears; but, with lots of care.

An artist she is, a violinist to the core,
An Argentinean by birth; Brazilian at heart,
Plays her best when it's folk lore,
Each time she plays, money comes by the cart.

She as I know is very humble and down to earth,
To this world as her parents, with love they bore,
It was a pleasure to know her story from birth,
Her music and this friend, in heart she does store.

Tears to the eyes her music brings,
Soulful the violin, tears through the air,
The music very mystical, the soul it does cringe,
And feels as though, one is in Gods own lair!

November 22nd 2013
In Bangalore

Sushrut

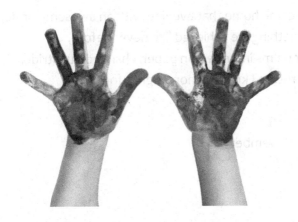

I went to school as a little child,
Dad left me once in that place all alone.
I screamed to no avail and I even cried,
But with time, it turned to be fun.

The kids were great and the teachers a pain,
The beginning was good, the time passed by,
I did not want to study, but I had to in vain
Everyone grilled me; I still reminisce, and do cry.

I remember when we learned to paint,
Colours in multitude, splattered on a plate,
All of us screamed, and in innocence quaint,
Splattered the colours with palms, yes it was great.

On a paper as our hands they fell,
Joy out of bounds we all then felt,
The first painting churned out I could smell,
Paint was fresh and on it our name we spelt.

We came home that evening with an awesome pride,
Something we achieved like never before,
Our palms inscribed on paper, changed our stride,
My future I knew it shone right afore.

16th November 2013

The Umbrella

It clings to a stalk poised in wait,
Two legs encircling fingers holding tight,
The third dangling but in a steady held poise,
The fourth up in the air holding the leaf

Well what is it waiting for, what's in sight?
A look beyond yonder its gazing eyes,
An insect humming buzzing in a dizzy flight,
The tongue tensed, waits for it, as it flies.

41

Succulent it is, as it just learnt to fly,
Nascent by birth, cracking the larval cocoon,
Stretching its wings, to soar as it does try,
Still juicy remnants of its birth sticking on

24th September 2013

One Last Time

Life severed, yes its true,
Just a few succulent drops,
Keeps me dragging on phew,
But God almighty tell me too,
My partner been pulled out, but, by who?

Cruelty even after being severed,
Seems rather painful to be separated
But God can we help these humans,
They seem so cruel, so uncaring; and,
Life to them does it really seem to matter!

Place: Harweel Site – PDO Oman
25th January 2012

Dream

Baring a cliff of bare rock on one side,
The deep blue sea endless on the other,
I waited bated breath, knew will come a tide; and,
So hope with a glimmer, a smile knew yonder,
A day would come when the moon would pull,
The magnetic waves of earth so much,
The sea would rise and move my dream,
Toss it with the winds of change; and,
Let it set sail once again!

PDO Harweel Site Office
21-01-2012

Tenderness

That Tenderness is normally great to feel,
It always feels as real with the wetness of rain,
It touches the depths of the soul; and as I before you
      kneel,
To say how much I mean, the feeling it drives away all
      my pain.

If ever I close my eyes, on you may it be forever,
God bless my heart let the rain be forever,
Well life is not so great but; every moment I wish to
      savour,
And make merry and feel great forever, forever.

Written on someone's face book page
in reply to one of their posting
August 28th, 2012
Harweel – Construction Site

Umasankar Vadrevu

A Letter to Myself

It was a long drawn afternoon on August Thirteen,
Into the bosses chamber we all were herded,
It did not in the slightest feel as if in routine,
As the room it felt more than over crowded.

I hate it when there is beating around the bush,
The mosquitoes are then normally pushed from Oblivion,
Felt as if we were each given to wear a tarboosh,
And we all felt sprayed by pesticide by an agrarian

Bloody hell come to the point was the consensus,
The sear could be felt through the cold afternoon sun,
I would have loved gifting him with the pungent
        asparagus,
Or sprayed him with bullets, of cringing words, of pun

Life surely did not seem very fair then,
But for a contracting engineer it's always on the edge,
Life isn't fair, it's dodgy and the back it did burn,
And felt as if it balanced itself, squarely on the ledge.

But then life, it cannot stop, for even a momentary notion,
The murk has to fall; the bucket list must be revisited,
Happiness and pain everything must be in motion,
A new job has to be sought, and the money bin
          repositioned.

August 14th 2012,
Harweel Camp

Left on The Right Path

The journey it beckons you forth a forest dense,
Twisting and winding through streams and rock,
Dark green and moist the trail actuates sense,
Devours loneliness, makes us run amok!

February 12th, 2012

Visions

He never witnessed a vision,
For a couple of hundreds of years, may be in ecstasy,
Although a few thousands were on a mission,
Was it grass or dope that made them go crazy!!

He was first at the temple seven years ago; and,
One could hear the dreary laments
Whilst the occurrence really concerns,
Of credulous creature's exploitations

He was disgusted by it all, though saw no miracles
A girl of fourteen did visions envisage,
125 years ago they say, at the temple
Pilgrim's visit with Gods own message

'The temple' stands as an example
In thousands of places of pilgrimage
Where miracles are 'performed'
Without much ado or damage

It always begins with individuals
Having a vision of the family,
In any religion mainly angels,
A mother or the lord himself the Holy!

The apparitions seen in visions are not neutral,
Most who surface do not come as mere bystanders?
All smiles and blessings, yes they do, as all men tell,
What they may and what they must do with fervor.

All personified visionaries assert,
That they are envoys from heaven with power,
To save, redeem and even destroy,
Infiltrate and dominate the brain of god's flowers

He went on pursuing his astronaut gods,
But could not forget the deep impression,
Every case arid, every place with visionaries
Unleash an unending procession

Whether the temple recognized the miracle,
Forbade it or merely endure it in silence.
Beliefs that they are blessed when it becomes hysterical
The humans who do so believe every occurrence

In what primitive soil does this faith nourish?
What evident eternal force makes it thrive?
Independent of space and time it does flourish
Untouched by religion the thought stays alive

In order to understand the phenomenon et al
One has to get to know the 'illusionaries'
Circumstances and places involved in all
And believe in people who have rosaries.

06-02-2012
PDO Harweel Site

Hope

As I sit here hands held tight,
Waiting to hear of a dream shatter,
Hope it doesn't happen tonight,
As I hold my heart safely in a platter.

Well times do change and hope not you,
I guessed and hoped that it won't be you,
But well life for me doesn't seem good,
You tell me how do you do.

Rhymes are something that matter no more,
My heart it moves, glides and does soar,
Love a lot in your life will downpour,
Only from the one and only despicable ME

PDO - Harweel Office Oman
23rd September, 2010

Life

Life I know will never be the same without you,
You came into my life as a passionate kiss,
Showed me the light,
And remained to stay,
I like your ways,
I liked your style,
I hoped in my heart,
And as I write now is my desire,
That one day we will be together,
To walk the aisles of mother earth,
The greenery shall be our path,
And the sky enveloped ground shall be our home,
But even in my dreams when I hear the sound of your
        footsteps,
I awaken waiting to hear you call out my name,
But alas I awaken to the deepest nights - frightened,
I sometimes wonder if you will ever be mine.

I know you are happy and a carefree soul,
Happiness encompassed,
With your most coveted friends,
My heart feels the compassion it has for you,
But dear I have allayed my fears to you,
When I sit to relax and my thoughts swing through your
        carefree thoughts,

I begin to get a feeling well...............................
I wish I were wrong,
But the sinking feeling never stops..........................
What seems normal or a casual thing for you,
In my deepest inner-self,
I know and I fear you may change,
And that day as now I will always wish,
And pray to GOD that you be a happy girl as I always did,
But fears, doubts and loneliness,
Feelings of pain and numbness, as they slowly grow,
Inching through to me as a growly big bear,
Will it subside, will it die,
Will my fears ever subside?

I sit here and as I write in a passionate flow,
It's been years since I wrote some lines,
Wish and pray that I do so,
More often than never again,
Show me the light and the path,
Free me from all inhumane paths,
I wish always to be a carefree bird,
To let my thoughts overflow in life,
To feel free I know is to be happy,
A crush for passion as I once had,
I only pray and wish in happiness and pain,
Since people don't stay long with me,
Please my poetry – Please never ever leave me.

September 13th 2010

Wormy Gorgeous

Lone Corridors
Closed doors
Offices open
None there
Vikas on duty
In the heat
A hushed voice
A whisper heard,
Eyes watching,
The lonely pair
A lonely ring,
The worm's wriggle,
Boring the earth!
And exclaims
Wormy Gorgeous!
Is that you!!!

July Twelfth, 1999

Worm

Worms infect your email,
As yet through channels unknown,
You better safe guard MS-Office
Word, excel, point and all.........,
Or else you'll one day be eaten,
Word by word and file by file,
And slowly......................
To other computers shall slowly set sail.
So read on and beware of the Worm!!

July Ninth, 1999

The First

It is always the first, who goes long,
Searching for new lands, but is never wrong,
Its better you don't search for him,
He has gone in search of a new song.

August Twenty Seventh, 1990

A Mirage

A road led on,
Once...........
On, on beyond
Now remains only
A breach; that,
Forever will remain,
Just a breach
Then it looked,
As though, well..............
But now, no more so,
Did that road
Lead...........on; yes,
Though it did,
But still feels as though,
It was all,
Just
A Mirage

July Ninth, 1990

ℐℕℒ

Of cards of paper I don't care,
What are they; just pamphlets bare
Friendship that I longed for,
In you to find................
Have I?
As I question myself
Again and again
Well have I?
A break...........certainly
On these long stretches wide,
As I trod on pebbles and stones,
Slipping at times
Groping for light
A twisted ankle
A broken thought
Well....................
It's just as it was before
Dark all around

May Twentieth, 1990

On the Class of Ninety

We came from far and wide,
We came from varied life styles,
But here under one roof, (KREC's hide),
We lived till we reached here mile by mile.

Here we came to have a strong base,
From no-man's land to a metallic one,
Here we felt and feel safe,
As time went on it was fun.

This is where each of us met,
All of us we the METS,
Cultivated in us a friendship class,
Which isn't as fragile as you think is glass

As the years went by, the bond strengthened,
Ordering and disordering was a continual process,
Strain hardening though at times present; But,
At all times were the super dislocations.

Major Reddy will be put to shame,
When it comes to camouflage,
In this class of twenty five,
The fairer sex is lost Oh, My!

Springtime Rhapsody

Piping rich with warm pep talk,
Sanjeev always boosted us
Cheerful and chirping diplomatic though,
Amit always made some fuss

Sundar sitting in the middle,
Preparing slogging for GRE
He never did with any one fiddle
Except the cute little poodle

When it comes to long legs,
Zinc and Anand are to name,
With his Shaktimaa.....an Trucks,
Anand has driven himself to fame.

One guy we needn't mention,
A class apart he stands,
Chewing the bottom half of his moustache,
He falls asleep on any land.

Lost souls aren't rare,
Occasionally in this class are there,
And come to class only,
When given shock waves

Pessimists, Ah! Them I hate; But,
What luck! He happens to be my project mate.
Cribs and cries all along,
That well really is fate.

Now comes the middle order men,
Capable to drive everyone crazy,
It's better to live in a coopered-ken
Than with people with rolls consecutive

Rankies aren't hard to search,
Headache or anything they take to books,
As I look yonder from my perch,
May be well I'm looking for hooks

As he seeks solace in the temple,
He says, "Lord please forgive my sins",
If not Durham N.C
Get me at least partial aid in Wisconsin.

While playing ball badminton, Govind has a soft touch,
Of games and Ashwin we needn't mention as such
I am sorry pals Ashok I don't know inside out
But leaving Sudhir will surely cause another bout.

The KREC flash federation, will surely realize its blunder,
In having called on Katts – The ultimate wonder
Gravy needs special mention, a master mind so great,
He's proved that victory and defeat, do not
        depend on fate

Springtime Rhapsody

I've left out K.T, but it's all by intention,
It'll take me a whole lot of space, all his talents to mention,
I've had my share of ills, "I can hear you tell,
But with happy memories my friends, I bid you a warm
farewell.

April Twenty Fifth, 1990

Memories of Your Childhood

Those lovely days of yours,
Haven't anywhere gone,
Sit back in your room
And thoughts when will unfurl
A moving picture
Of those bygone days
That you have loved so much
Will again unfurl

Those sights and smells,
Those made your mother yell
Or of all the boys in town
Who had an eye on you?
For what you were then
I guess innocent and sweet
Don't go out alone
Though a thousand times told,
Did you not at least once
Into the dark night adventure
If not alone at least,
With a friend,
In whom you did trust

Springtime Rhapsody

Where is my freedom
And my carefree mood
As I see you ask
They haven't in one swift motion
With your childhood gone,
Passed away as you put it
Gone, forgotten! Is it all lost
No they haven't
But are there,
Which in time will revert
Back to their original state
So far only of the past,
You've given a thought,
One look into the future
And you'll know it for sure

When you shall
After your marriage beget,
A cute little girl,
Like you were once (It's not that you aren't now)
Then those days
Which you think are lost
Shall once again
Come back

March Twenty Eighth, 1990
Reply to a poem written by a junior in the
Karnatakian 89', "Memories of My Childhood"

A Letter to A Friend

Here is just another day,
Try and make it go your way
If not don't just cry
That could be your fate, by and by,
That isn't that my little girl
What are you but a lovely pearl?
All your hair in splendid curls,
I guess you will be taken by an earl.
In slow seconds does time go,
Once though in reach now no more so.
Why not come into my arms now
Later on don't ask how.

March Seventh, 1989

Nature

These spring nights,
One can smell violets,
Crisp cool air
Sweet scented nature
As it lulls us into,
Its lap's lovely ....soft,
Through another journey
Into Eternity

January Twenty Seventh, 1990

. . . .

As I look down far below
My eyes searching rest on a forbidden plough,
A twist a turn on these roads...........
On which was once a quest,
And was then thought to be
In life the best

As time flew by
With these lengthening years
Those happy thoughts that once were,
Now remain as tears

As the bitter thoughts keep coming,
And I wishing the past slowly fade,
To fill it up with happy lines,
To make it an everlasting glade

So pure and clear
Breeze on a winter day,
Whispering to the leaves and bark bare
Joys of yet another bay

Springtime Rhapsody

Seawards yes, with a gentle swing,
Carried in the sweet scented air
Go all my thoughts slowly
Into the deep blue lair

December Seventeenth, 1989

Alabaster

White
Yes, Alabaster white,
Riding,
A bicycle on your way back
He saw you midway
Asked you if,
Poetry you do write,
As before

Answered
What you did,
He remembers not.
Sad isn't it, he was asleep
Dreamt .... and,
You he saw,
In Alabaster White,
Late Last Night

November Nineteenth, 1989

Chrysanthemum

Pearly white,
A chocolate layer,
Her face so bright,
Like a flower
A Chrysanthemum,
Pinkish white,
A lot of yum,
For everyone
From my perch
On the western front
As my eyes do search,
And finally rest
On the beautiful bust
Besides whom is sitting a pest.

November Fifteenth, 1989

Crush

Into my heart,
You stepped that day
Leaving footsteps
While on way
I still wonder the way you felt
I then thought you were God sent,
So beautiful and great,
Like an Indian "Chaste",
From that day on.............
Attracted to you I'm some how
The pretty face and the smile
Pretty cute you've got a style

September Twenty Second, 1989

Jog Falls

Climbing down
In quick rhythmic steps
All converging
To the one place
Eye catching
Beautiful
Mentioned .... No
I haven't seen before
The falls
Coming down in a fast trot
That's why it's called
The Jog Falls

September Tenth, 1989
At Jog Falls

In A Letter To A Friend

Letters I've written enough,
And I'm tired of writing another,
I do not expect one from you,
Never again in this life ever

Times do change and they have to
People have problems with their ego, Phew!
Now the time is yours to choose
You've chosen ego, I've got the cue

I sometimes begin to wonder,
What on earth you're doing,
As such a rare specimen,
I doubt, if I'll find another

Receiving letters from you is a dream,
Which even the best dreamer can't dream of,
I had patiently waited for one from you,
Now no more I do hope, nor even hope to

May Sixteenth, 1989

Letter to Yamuna

I thought to write a poem on you,
So beautiful and chaste so much you,
Words, words, they flow keying in,
An eternal mystery a map before me

Your time, my time, hobby time,
I miss you, yes I do all the time
Too many rhymes don't sound nice; but,
I haven't yet got a starting line.

Your face a wonder always dear,
So pure and sweet like a pear,
I don't want to see on that face a tear,
I've never willed, nor will ever.

You were to me a mystery,
The day you left us, looked as though forever,
I have always wondered and asked dad why,
Uncle ever got a transfer.

Dad said, "Son that's life"; and,
You're just beginning to see it all,
How I hoped it'd all change; and,
Hoped to see your pretty face again

I've always seen the harder part of things,
Ever since we last saw you,
May be God willed it just that way,
It seemed as though, it's all unfair.

Times do change and sure they'll,
I'll come to see you in September,
Shocked and surprised you surely will be,
Don't then hide behind your mother, dear

Things have changed and will continue to,
When will you be writing a letter or two,
Suresh told me, that you haven't changed,
Since the time when I saw you last

This I'm writing to you from the class,
I wonder how much longer, I'll withstand the blast,
This man shouts at the top of his voice,
He is a pain for all us metallurgists

Ah! The class is nearly coming to an end,
Just another quarter of an hour or so,
I then will go to the post office,
And post a letter to my home

May Ninth, 1989
In a letter to Yamuna Swamiappan

Letter To N.K. Kiran (3)

Birthdays have come and so will have gone,
Never will one so drab without fun,
As thoughts of the far away keep coming on
I doubt if this I shall even reckon.

I always thought a rendezvous perhaps,
Around the corner a treat in the offing,
All that was left for me were scraps,
Of a great friendship another sad happening

Blooming in the shade, luxuriant growth,
Satisfaction utmost, pleasant to breathe,
Shared but once, thoughts lovingly,
To open up now seems far from eternity

The shade not as complete as before,
But with spots of speckled sunshine,
Adulterated with the thoughts of another sphere,
Enquiring if reconciled friendship will ever last

February Twenty Seventh, 1990

A Confession

He stole into my room, one day,
And told me something,
That he'd never tell me,
Had I been wide awake

As I sat a few minutes ago,
In the library reading the paper,
A stifling wave (of remorse) swept over me,
Guilty I was and now I am at your bedside

These were the things he said,
Think over and over was I,
And guilt so overtook me,
That here I am at your bedside.

I had been angry; and,
Scolded as you were dressing for school,
'Cos you merely dabbed your face,
And bothered not to clean your shoes

Faults at breakfast did I find,
Not one but probed for more,
As you spilled some and gulped the rest,
Frowning I said, "God, when will he really learn".

Springtime Rhapsody

As I came up the road from work,
(I spied and), playing marbles you were on your knees,
Holes in your stocking did I find,
Firing I sent you into the house.

Later when I was reading,
I remember how you came in timidly,
Glancing over my paper, irritated,
"What is it you want", snapped I.

Then you ran across me in one tempestuous plunge,
Threw your arms around my neck,
They tightened slowly with affection,
Which god had set blooming in your heart

That which god had set blooming in your heart,
Which neglect even could not wither,
You kissed me, my good night kiss,
And were gone, pattering up the stairs

Then shortly afterwards,
The paper slipped,
When a sick feeling came over,
I wondered what habit was doing to me?

Of finding fault of reprimanding,
Though small you are,
I expected too much,
A measure by the yardstick of my own years

Umasankar Vadrevu

I am sorry son, and;
Beside your bed I now kneel,
Telling you how ashamed I've been,
Confessing all, to you my boy
Now that you are fast asleep

February Twenty Third, 1989,
My father and Me

Farewell, My Friend

It was hard to say goodbye,
To friends such as you
But since you then were leaving,
There was not much else to do
Except pray that god will bless,
As you travel along life's ways,
To wish you good health and,
Happiness, increasing day by day,
Hoping you take these blessings,
And that you will be in touch,
I said farewell my friend,
And remember you are missed very much.

February Fifteenth, 1989

My Days At KTC

My days at KTC,
Have nearly come to an end,
I remember those days,
When we first did meet,
Friendship grew; and,
Closer we became,
As the days went by,
Each time we met,
We talked like we knew each other,
For a long, long time

I remember each of you,
So distinctly so clear,
A place I kept aside,
For all the seven of you,
Seven I feel really
Is a number real unlucky?
For first the youngest dropped out,
In whose place came another new
The new guy stayed not long
Nor an impression lasting
Did he create

Hardly two months of classes
We had,
When we started thinking,
Of a vacation,
Padma was the first,
And asked, "Ma'am can we have one",
We were thankful, though,
Didn't express it openly

The holidays were over,
Classes began.
Ravi dropped out saying,
"Machha, I have to prepare, (for the exams)
Time went on; and,
November came,
When realization struck,
That it's time,
To study for the same

Classes continued
With breaks in the middle,
Finally closed down on November 15,
And our labs,
By then had just begun
Labs continued and theory came,
Everything completed,
And home we went.

Holidays we had,
Till January Fifth,
But only I went,
After the twenty sixth,
Oh! Then what a fate,
Had to go every day,
Just to make up
All alone,
During those hot summer days

January Twenty Third, 1989

On primarily,
Ma'am: Mrs. S.A. Furtado
Ravi Kumar T., Madhav Kalyan,
M.V. Satyan, Ms. Padma Kamath,
Ms. Parinitha Punja; Myself

Travelling can be fun,
If travelled by a new train,
Or every time you passed this way,
It would be a real pain.

Stopping by the stations same,
Every time this way you came,
No I thought never again,
Will I travel by a slow train?

Painful they turn out to be,
Stopping at stations unknown,
They begin to remake history,
That's how the Indian railways
Make a centenary

January Ninth, 1989

Umasankar Vadrevu

The Arampur Widows

Nestling along the banks of Bidda,
Where flow the mighty distributary of Ganga,
They snake their way through Sunderban's,
Till they reach the village whose roofs glint golden.

The Sun rays pierce through the lifting fog,
Like dozens of spotlights in the dark,
A plaintive cry from a nearby bog
And the morning air resounds to the Koel's call,

A wet wind rises from the waters and spreads,
Through the vegetation of mixed trees,
Lotuses bob up and down,
Like sails afloat on a bed of green

The old folks cough; While,
The women stroke their hearths,
And something's really wrong,
As the men have gone very far

In the village the women wait,
They wait for a week and at times more,
She feeds her children, scrubs her hut,
And prays for her husband's safe return

She waits on and on till the day's up,
And then she looks on for the next day,
Finally when he doesn't turn up,
She realizes she's just another one.

Written some time in 1987
II BE Metallurgy
(Sent back by Vijay Shanbhag)

Advanced Acclaim for
"Springtime Rhapsody"

"Springtime Rhapsody takes us through the authors own world from time immemorial to the present day time in his own steady gait. Poetical words magically intertwine thoughts into words; showing that there is always a different way to interpret a topic. Dip into this book from anywhere; a new tale arises. Re-think the way you would have thought about a topic or a photograph, send this poet a line and see a new angle emerge in the poets own words."

- DR. SANGEETA PARMEKAR DEVERAPALLI,
  CHIEF ANESTHESIOLOGIST, OMEGA HOSPITALS,
  HYDERABAD, ANDHRA PRADESH, INDIA

"Words from daily life perfectly knit into his woven perception of the present world. Expressions, feelings and thoughts have that magical touch in every one of his poems, a thought provoking read to understand how differently everyone can think."

- DR. SRINAGESH PODURI, MBBS DPH FRACGP,
  GENERAL PRACTIONER AUSTRALIA
  EX. DEPUTY CHIEF MEDICAL DIRECTOR (PUBLIC
  HEALTH); SOUTH CENTRAL RAILWAYS, INDIA

Introducing the Young Gaurika Mehrotra and her Poems

About the Poet

Gaurika Mehrotra

Passionate to write, bubbly in thoughts this little girl writes with ease. She is such a wonderful little poet to speak to! It sometimes amazes the way this little girl thinks and puts words to her thoughts. At a time when most children play outdoors this girl prefers to write poems and stories weaving a little world of her own. An adept story teller and a poetess!

The Royal Cook

The Royal Cook of the palace
Her name was Miss Alice
She did cook lovely dishes
Which mostly consists of egg and fishes?
She cooked seven courses
From all sort of sources
But of course her specialty
Which she served with royal hospitality
And guess what...it were sweets
She surely cooked it better than meats
She wouldn't let a single speck of dirt
Sit on her shirt
And when she would be done with cooking the dishes
She would gobble up half the fishes
Without salt or butter
And then she would mutter...
I ate too much to bear
Oh No! God! This is not fair
The Royal Cook of the palace
Her name was Miss Alice

Gaurika Mehrotra
Age 9
April 10th, 2015
Bangalore

Have You Ever Tried Catching A Cloud?

I did one day,
But when I tried, it only
Flew away

Into the sea,
Along the mist
High in the sky
The wind it kissed

It flew and flew
Far away from me
But left behind no clue

Then for a minute it ceased itself,
High up in the sky
Like a hanging wooden shelf
Then again it went by

This time racing faster
Than it usually did
Like a racing master
Faster than any other kid

Then suddenly I realized
I had collected it in my Jar!
But then I also realized
That I had left the Jar ajar!

Have you ever tried catching a cloud?
I did one day
But when I tried, it only
Flew away

Gaurika Mehrotra
Age 9
Dec 07th, 2015
Bangalore

My Magic Pencil is the Best

It is not a type of magic where
If you drop a picture it will come alive
Or if you write a wish it comes true
But my memories and love are in it
My magic pencil is the best.

Gaurika Mehrotra
Age 9
Aug 17th, 2014
Bangalore

Painter in the Sky

There is a painter in the sky
Don't ask me why
She paints the sky blue
And then the cows moo
She paints the Sun yellow
And all the children say Hello
She paints the night
As the children get a fright
And then eats her dinner
Which is a cheese pie
She is happy her work is done
Then she forgets to paint the Sun!

Gaurika Mehrotra
Age 9
Nov, 2015
Bangalore

The Day My Tooth Shook

Oh Dear! My tooth shook
That means dentist to take a look
I say I better read a book
Oh no it pains!
But mummy said if you don't go I'll hit you with a cane
I wish it would rain
So Daddy couldn't take me
I say I better make some tea
Or get stung by a bee
At last it fell
And then I yell.

Gaurika Mehrotra
Age 9
Nov 11th, 2014
Bangalore

The Grey Sky

It was a sunny day
I was out on my way
To the sky which was grey
It was the month of May
As I was walking and talking
Which I usually do
While eating pumpkin stew
I noticed a staircase
That seemed like a mystery case
Was in my way
Which led to the sky which was grey
Then I looked carefully
And I saw a park to play
It was no more a sunny day
At night fell...
I tell you the tale of today
The sky was no more Grey
It was a lovely day!

Gaurika Mehrotra
Age 9
Oct, 2014
Bangalore

Umasankar Vadrevu

The Little Poet

There was a boy who loved to
Write poems all the time
But they never rhymed
Oh! How hard he tried
He never got it right
He was very rude
And said, I hate myself dude

Gaurika Mehrotra
Age 9
Aug 17th, 2015
Bangalore

102

The Robbery

The watchman was snoring
The bank was in trouble
The robbers were pouring
Money like it was rubble
Not a word would they mumble
While taking the cash
For they could stumble
As it was kept in a stash
Straight the money was poured into sacks
Into a car they were 35 lacs
Down the robbers drove to the city
They were all tired
But it was a pity
As the watchman was fired

Gaurika Mehrotra
Age 9
May 26th, 2015
Bangalore

To A Friend

You're an amazing friend
To this friendship there is no end
You always share all your things
And on my face a smile it brings
A great friend? Yes you are.
Your friendship has lasted quite far
Your smile is so fragile
How can I forget to tell?
Now let's get to the point and make
It very clear
You're my friend
But everyone's dear

Gaurika Mehrotra
Age 9
June 29th, 2015
Bangalore

Printed in the United States
By Bookmasters

M@dness
and
Musings

M@dness
and
Musings

SCARLETT PRAGYA

Contents

About the Poet

Scarlett Pragya

A highly opinionated, tongue-in-cheek poet that wears sass on her sleeves and high heels. A graduate in International Relations from University of Queensland, she is now studying Social Work in Australia. She calls herself an atheist, idealist, and a humanist whose right arm is inked, 'drunk on poetry'. She loves libraries, smell of old books, double-decker boat ferries, late night long drives, hopelessly karaoking everywhere, cloud watching and working out for her newly forming abs. She writes because kidnapping people to act out her interesting make-believe worlds is technically illegal.

Nothingness

Atoms of my thoughts ripple
as I bathe myself
into the void of darkness.
Nothingness is bliss.

Shedding the paradigm of reality
and bringing fiction to life
inexplicable desires,
strange dreams wrought
stagnation, apathy, and entropy.
This world is a Paradox.

A flame dances seductively
enshrouding a corner of darkness
I am searching escape
in life and in death.
Deforming into nothingness.

Another Man

Give me another man!
Give me another man!
This time better, muscular
And with improved brain.
I shall put him to test
Take him down to taste the dirt
Of the dark abyssal shell.
Seal him with the kiss -
Cold as death, and hot as hell.
Suck him into the delirium of love
Bind his body, numb his thoughts
Till into one pleasure and pain dissolve.
And after I am done,
I will put a curse on his vain.
No woman would then want him,
And I will go for another man.

Sublime Love

In the ocean of unknown
A lighthouse erected
All fears surrendered
Despair crawled back
Mermaids no longer sang
The songs of doom
But then I let you go
Kissed goodbye to a love sublime
And now I happily watch you
Screwing up someone else's life
Instead of mine

Stigma

Stained with sins
She dragged the chains
Of her past

Laced in lies
She swallowed the curses
And ruthless remarks

Rusted with regrets
She repented her existence
To endless extent

Searing in Shame
She towed the weight
Of her soul

The Stigma?
Oh, an audacious attempt
To Breakout

The stagnant circle of traditions
Stinking of suffocating beliefs
To a world

.

Where she can stand for
What she dreams
What she is

Hybrid

When I grow up...
I want to be a werewolf
Run and hunt, naked
Howl at the world in dark nights
Roam in daylight in sheep's disguise.

When I grow up...
I want to be a creepy spider
Vicious, nasty, with hideous claws
From murky woods where gloom tolls
Crawl into the safe homes
Scare off little girls sleeping with dolls.

When I grow up...
I only want to be swollen in pride
Of being brown testicles under the pants
Oh, the power and freedom and power
Owning scotch, women, and no shame

5

Cocktails, Cleavages, and Confusions

He can see
The black and red
Cocktail dresses
Cleavages on display
Exchanging and enchanting
For the purpose
Which no one knows of
In the shadows
Where the words are drawn
After the trees shed their
Last spring flowers
World makes sense
With men and women
Inebriated

Morning Solitude

The morning light sweeps
Through the cold glass
Dispelling the dark on my face
And in my heart
This timeless moment: my moment
I claim it with all I am
Dreams dance in lazy hazy eyes
Tangled in the curls of my hair
Vague memories sweetly ache
To bathe in sunshine
I feel in no part of your world
Is there a trace of me
I wish to lie still.
Soaking solitude.
When I become a part of the world
I finally understand
That moment was all I ever had.

Love's Labyrinth

The dark silhouette of a cold heart
Slumbers in a grey garden
Where the dead crow was buried
To mark the sign of a love lost.

So now you are back, all changed
Darling, I could only love so much
My love is a labyrinth of peril
And I am the mistress of Hell's devil.

A Place to Go

The smoke of cigarette
Round and round it goes
Just like the misery
Of this young man.

And few packs of Whiskey
To accompany his story
Speeds past the roads of a city
That waits for none.

Got nowhere to go
More speed, more smoke
Curses fate, curses all
Lights blind and he chokes.

Jobless, clueless, continues to ride
Just a hit and a crash
And now he has got
A place to go!

Scarlett Pragya

The Canvas

I remember when I was where
- or what I was when
But I wish I knew then
What I know now.

I gaze at the canvas –
Painted with the hues
of memories;
of mirages;
of dreams drenched in frost
- hung above the fire place.

And the life fumes above
Through the chimney

What's Up?

Timeless desperation is up
The noses of people
That mindlessly go to and fro
Every road, every steeple.

Praying, crying, begging –
You eye on what's not yours
Take peeks under lifted skirts
Everyday nine to four.

I will tell you what is up –
When you ask me 'What's up today?'
'Honey, your time and my underpants,'
And they are fucking staying that way.

A Medley in Observation

And here I sit again, cross-legged
Put on the same old nostalgic song to play
In the background, a vanilla candle flickers
With an intent to pour out some honesty
And write a poetry that will tell you
How I look upon the world wide eyed
A charade, beyond my understanding
As beyond as my control over my own life choices
Oh, how we are but hilariously complicated specks
On the faces of Earth, alternating the selves
Between playing the pawn, then being the player
Being quarter true, half lie, show and pretend
And boy, does that medley ever end!

The Unnamed Madness

You think you know me, but you are mistaken.
You cannot know me until you have felt
the feeling of tearing your clothes apart.

That aggression of wrecking
everything you could see,
you could smell, you could sense.

When you know the new day
that will dawn will only bring upon
the nightmares you buried in the grave.

You starve for the clouds of anger to clear.
But instead it thunders.

It pours all over you like never before
and you join the army of darkness
and you feel it stomping all over your body.

You have never felt this ugliness before
and you take ugly, unnamed pride in it.
It's hideous; you don't want anyone to see your face.
Every breath that you gasp for, consumes you down
the black hole of your blind, bland thoughts.

But this is true, this is you at your scary bay.
And your madness, your ugliness, are here to stay.

A Nightmare

I had a dream
To not be forgotten
'Twas such a night
My love, you came back
To me, and I woke up
In absolute fright

The Unsung Song

Oh the midnight mania
Don't I love it
Don't I crave it
The fresh peach
and wild ripe apricot
Slides down my throat
The thoughts stir
The vision blurs
Consume me
Drown me
So yes I am numb
So yes I am drunk
Do you care?
Will you dare?
'cause I am stuck
Don't give a fuck
Your offer- I will pass
And dance to the jazz
How often do you boast
For being crazy and lost
All the rules I do bend
Take me where it all ends
The madness, the confessions
The pain, the obsession

Scarlet Pragya

I carve my heart out and stab it
Nail it, burn it, bury it
My poem is drunk
And my song, unsung

An Autumn Tree

The autumn leaves flutter
Their fate to the ground
Joys fall, shades fade
Winnowing wind whirls around

Once mirth filled nests
Dry and lie in desolation
Is the Earth giving away
A glimpse of my destination?

Taste of tears amalgamate
With the wine of pain's delight
Distress of nature invariably
Tranquillizes my heart's plight

Earth has been forsaken of soul
Aching in fruitless rhyme and reason
Soulless me – soulless Earth coexist
in the conspiracy of sadistic season

Life drawls a lonely song
Away the pleasures, desires stride
Still hopeful, I wait as I wither
With a tree that lost its pride.

Last Wait

The dark night lurks
Above the empty wide road
The flickering lamp post
Sizzles my shadow
Eyes stare out to the far end
I stand, wait, and anticipate
Wrapped in my old overcoat
Under the clouds of contemplation
Stretched over the sky of
Screaming life

Overture

Bland wine, blue sky, blank face
Each day, the rising immortal sun
Pushes the hope to summit

Sun-glazed, it shines for a while
Each night, it then falls from the grace
Broken, stripped, shattered

The Tragedy

To drown your name
One glass after another
I filled to the brim.

Oh little did I know
Your name knew
How to swim!

Belief

Sometimes I wish
To soar up high
Leave my forlorn being
Shed the weight
So that the laws of men
No longer work on me
And gravity
Neither pulls me down
I can rest in the clouds
Then pour down on ocean
As rain
Let my breaths descend
in the turquoise blue
Then for years
Rest in isolation
Like a dormant seed
Waiting to crack open
When the world is asleep
Sometimes I wish
To forever sink in my musings
Sans wisdom
Wonder and wander
Alas, my behest is shunned
For it is illicit
in the eyes of realism

Scarlett Pragya

An Ode to the Poet Within

One of these days I will break
When I write my fingers shake
No more can I stall
The opaque wall
Never let me see through
I was afraid to know the truth
The sweet bliss of lies
Kept me alive
Every road I ever took
I never thought it through
Can you return to me?
I long for you
I crave for you
In sunny days and starry nights
In darkness and in light
I once found you
And I bound you
Now I want you
To find me
Please find me
Please bind me
I dug you out of red grave
It is your time and turn now
I only want to be saved.